S0-BNV-834

Breathe like a Bear

30 Mindful Moments for Kids to Feel Calm and Focused Anytime, Anywhere

Kira Willey

Illustrated by Anni Betts

Text copyright © 2017 by Kira Willey
Cover art and interior illustrations copyright © 2017 by Anni Betts

All rights reserved. Published in the United States by Rodale Kids, an imprint of
Random House Children's Books, a division of Penguin Random House LLC, New York.
Originally published in hardcover in the United States by Rodale Kids, an imprint of
Rodale Books, Emmaus, PA, in 2017.

Rodale and colophon are registered trademarks and Rodale Kids is
a trademark of Penguin Random House LLC.

Visit us on the Web! rhcbooks.com

Educators and librarians, for a variety of teaching tools, visit us at
RHTeachersLibrarians.com.

Library of Congress Cataloging-in-Publication Data is available upon request.
ISBN 978-1-62336-885-2 (hardcover) — ISBN 978-1-62336-884-5 (ebook) —
ISBN 978-1-62336-883-8 (pbk.)

MANUFACTURED IN CHINA
10 9 8 7 6
First Edition

Random House Children's Books supports the First Amendment and celebrates
the right to read.

For the children of
Donegan Elementary School,
who always greet me
with hugs and smiling faces.

Contents

v

Foreword

Do you ever feel like the children in your life could use a little help calming themselves down? Or maybe they need guidance learning how to focus or how to find positive energy. Mindfulness, the practice of being fully in the moment, is the answer. When kids discover that they're in control of their bodies through their breath, they can move to a state of awareness and positivity anytime, anywhere.

How we teach our kids this essential and life-enhancing skill is a question that Kira Willey answers in *Breathe Like a Bear*. Kira's mindfulness exercises are simple, fun, and incredibly engaging. Kids (and their grownups) will love doing these activities.

Children who practice mindfulness are better able to self-regulate, have improved social skills, sleep better, and demonstrate higher self-esteem—and this is just the beginning of all the positive effects. There's also increased focus, decreased anxiety and depression, and greater levels of academic achievement.

Chances are, if your family is anything like mine, the adults will begin doing these exercises even when the kids aren't around. They're just *that* catchy and enjoyable. And the beauty of Kira's work is that they can be done anywhere—in the car, in the classroom, at home, or even on the soccer field!

Set the tone for focus, calm, and positive energy with the child in your life—or your own inner child—by diving into the practices of this captivating book.

Michelle Kelsey Mitchell
*Cofounder of YoKid and
the National Kids Yoga Conference*

Introduction

When we pause and take a few deep breaths before reacting in just about any situation, things usually go better, right? If you're a parent or teacher, I'm sure you agree. Imagine if we could teach this critical skill of self-regulation to children very early in life. What more valuable skill could we give them?

Our children are growing up in a turbulent world. Add in packed schedules and the pressures of school and homework, and stress and anxiety are often the result. And the more kids are exposed to technology, the more disconnected they can feel from themselves.

The easy and fun mindfulness practices in this book will help young kids develop self-awareness, improve focus, release anxiety, and stretch their imaginations. Simple questions like, "What kind of cloud do you feel like today?" help them get in touch with their emotions in a fun and age-appropriate way.

Pick a few favorites to learn, and do them whenever (and wherever) they fit into your daily life. Maybe you try "1-2-3 Clap!" to get energized each morning, and "Today I'm Going to Be . . . " to set a positive intention for the day ahead. You might do "Candle Breath" at bedtime as a calming way to end the day. In the classroom, you could try "Rainstorm" to focus your students' attention before diving into a lesson, or "Send Good Thoughts" to teach compassion. And if you and your kids do these together, you're getting the benefits as well!

Mindfulness doesn't have to be complicated. You don't need a meditation cushion, chimes, or incense of any kind! And there's no need to go into lengthy explanations with kids about why mindfulness is good for you. In fact, the fewer words, the better. Just start breathing like a bear together, and see what happens.

I'd love to hear how you're using this book, so please get in touch! You can find me at kirawilley.com.

Do you ever feel a little, well, hyper? Like you have ants in your pants? It can be really hard to calm down sometimes. These exercises are easy and fun, and they'll help you settle your mind and your body so that you feel calm and peaceful. You can do these as many times as you like, and you might even want to try your favorite one with your eyes closed. Before you start, sit up tall and hold your body still.

Candle Breath

Imagine you're holding a candle.

Take a long breath in, and slooowly blow
the air out toward your candle.

You want to make your candle flame wiggle, but . . .
DON'T BLOW IT OUT!

Long breath in, slooow breath out.

Long breath in, slooow breath out.

Long breath in . . . now blow your candle out!

Aaahhh . . .

Hot Chocolate

Imagine you're holding a cup of hot chocolate in your hands.

It's much too hot to take a sip, so you need to blow on it to cool it off.

Bring your cup up close to you, take a long breath in, and slowly blow the air out, to cool off your hot chocolate.

Take another long breath in, and slowly blow the air out.

Now take a tiny little sip of your hot chocolate, and say "Mmmmm . . . !"

Make the "mmm" sound last as long as you can.

Try it again! Take a tiny little sip and say, "Mmmmmm . . ."

Put your hot chocolate down, take a long breath in, and let the air all the way out.

yum!

Flower Breath

Imagine a flower in front of you.

It's the most beautiful flower you've ever seen.

Can you see all the colors of the flower in your mind?

Imagine how it smells.

Take a long sniff in through your nose, and let all the air out through your mouth.

Take another long sniff in through your nose, and let all the air out through your mouth.

Take another long breath in,
and let it all the way out!

Count to Five

Have you ever heard someone say, "Let's take five?"

It means to take a quick break from what you're doing, and it's a great way to *CALM DOWN.*

As you breathe in, think ONE . . . TWO . . . THREE . . . FOUR . . . FIVE.

Now breathe out, and think ONE . . . TWO . . . THREE . . . FOUR . . . FIVE.

Try it again! Breathe in, and think ONE . . . TWO . . . THREE . . . FOUR . . . FIVE.

Breathe out, and think ONE . . . TWO . . . THREE . . . FOUR . . . FIVE.

Whenever you're mad or upset, try to remember to "take five."

It can help you feel calm and peaceful.

3 4 5

Bear Breath

Pretend you're a bear, hibernating for the winter.

When bears hibernate, they breathe **Slooowly**,
in and out through their noses.

Take a long breath in through your nose,
and let it all the way out.

Take another long breath in through your
nose, and let it all the way out.

Feel how cozy and safe you are
in your bear cave.

Take one more really long,
slow breath in through your nose,
and let it all the way out.

Your Favorite Color

What is your favorite color?

Is it blue, **purple**, orange, or **red**? Or another color?

Imagine a little ball of your favorite color inside your body.

Maybe it's where your heart is, or maybe it's in your belly.

Take a big breath in, and imagine the ball getting bigger and bigger. It takes over your whole body!

Imagine that everything all around you is your favorite color, and it feels really warm and good.

Take a long, slow breath in, and let it all the way out.

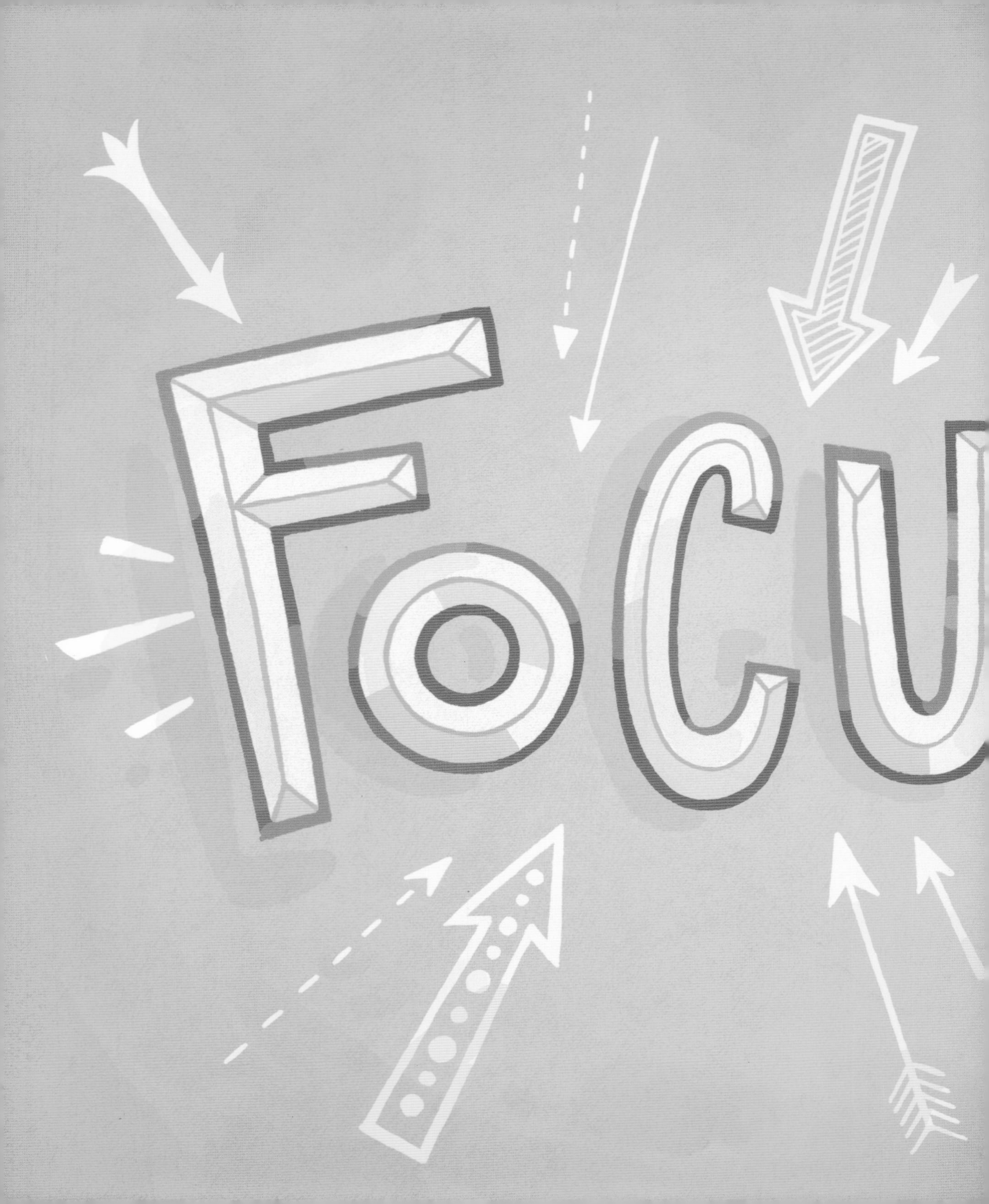
FOCU

When there's something we have to do, it can be really hard to pay attention to just *that one thing*. It's not easy to focus our minds on something without getting distracted. But with practice, our minds get better and better at it. These exercises are fun and quick, and they'll help your brain learn to concentrate. Before starting each one, sit up tall and take a deep breath. When you learn them, you might want to pick a favorite that you can practice any time you need to focus!

Rainstorm

Uh-oh, I think it might rain!

Rub your hands together to make the sound of the wind picking up.

Now tap your hands slowly on your lap—it's starting to rain!

Get faster and faster—now it's pouring!
We're going to get soaked!

Lightning! Clap your hands up high!
Thunder! Stomp your feet!
Lightning! Clap your hands up high!
Thunder! Stomp your feet!

Tap those hands on your lap again—it's really raining!

Now start to slow them down...I think the rain might be stopping...

Rub your hands together to make the sound of the wind...

Slooow it down,

slooow it down, and stop.

Everything is still and quiet.

Snake Breath

Let's do snake breath!

Make your mouth into the shape of a little "o."
Take a long breath in, like you're breathing through a straw.

As you let it out, hiss like a snake.

Take another long breath in, like you're breathing through a straw.

As you let it out, hiss like a snake. Make the "ssss" sound last as long as you can!

Try it one more time! Take a loooong breath in, and hissssss on the way out.

Sit up tall, take another long breath in, and just let it all the way out.

Waves on the Water

Imagine you're standing in front of a lake.

The water is flat and calm, like glass.

You have a stone in your hand, and you throw it in the water.

When it lands, it makes little waves on the water.

In your mind, watch the little waves as they go farther and farther out, getting smaller and smaller.

Watch the lake in your mind until it gets totally calm and flat again.

Take a long breath in, and let it all the way out.

Be a Bumblebee

Sit up tall as you can, and let's be bumblebees!

Make bumblebee wings by sticking your elbows out to the sides.

Wiggle your wings all around, and flap them up and down.

Take a big breath in, and **buzzzzzzz** as you let it out. Make the buzzzzz last as long as you can!

Now make big circles in the air with your bumblebee wings. Make circles one way, and then make circles the other way.

Take a big breath in, and *buzzzzzzz* as you let it out.

Now shake out your wings, take another long breath in, and let it all the way out!

Listen!

Sit up tall, take a long breath in, and let it all the way out.

Hold your body really still.

Listen.

What do you hear?

Close your eyes for a minute so you can really focus.

What sounds are around you?

If you listen even more, what do you hear?

Take a long breath in, and let it all the way out.

Where Is Your Breath?

Sit up tall, shake your body out a little bit, and then hold still.

Take a long breath in, and let it all the way out. Keep taking long breaths in and long breaths out.

Think about where you feel the air in your body.

Do you feel it in your nose or your mouth?

Your chest or your belly? Your left pinky toe?

In your mind, follow the air as it comes into your body and goes back out again.

Breathe in, breathe out.

Breathe in, breathe out. Where do you feel the air?

Take one more long breath in, and just let it all the way out.

*O*ur imaginations are sooo powerful. You can go *anywhere you want* in your mind. And you can *be* anything you want! But our imaginations need exercise to stay healthy, just like our bodies do. These fun exercises are a great workout for your imagination. And they'll help you remember to be kind and think about others, too. When you find one you really like, you can do it as many times as you want!

Clouds

Imagine you're a cloud in the sky.

What kind of a cloud are you?

Are you a white fluffy cloud?

Or a dark gray storm cloud? If you are, imagine your angry raindrops just falling away.

Maybe you're a silly cloud, making shapes of jellybeans and polar bears.

Or maybe you're a sparkly cloud, full of snowflakes!

You can be any kind of cloud you want.

Take a long breath in, and let it all the way out.

Kindness

Think of something kind you've done for someone.

Maybe you helped someone in your family with something at home, or you helped a friend at school.

Think of something kind that someone else did for you.

How did it make you feel?

Now, think of something kind that you haven't done yet, but you will, the next time you have the chance.

Is there someone you could help, or say some kind words to?

Try to remember to do that kind thing when you can!

Imagine You're a Tree

Imagine you're a tree.

You have roots growing down into the earth, holding your trunk steady and strong.

Your branches are reaching up high.

What kind of tree are you?

You can be any kind of tree you want.

Decide what color leaves you have, what your branches look like, and how tall you are.

See your whole tree in your mind.

Remember, your tree has strong roots that hold you safely in the ground, and strong branches that reach up toward the sky!

Send Good Thoughts

Think of someone you love, and imagine that person is standing in front of you.

Think of something really nice you could say to that person.

Say it quietly, in your mind.

Now think of a different person. Someone you don't know as well. Or maybe someone who's having a hard time right now.

Imagine that person is standing in front of you.

Think of something really nice you could say to that person.

Say it quietly, in your mind.

Take a long breath in, and let it all the way out.

Create Something New

It's time to invent something brand new in your mind.

Inventing means to create something no one's even thought of yet!

What will you invent? Hmmm . . .

See your invention in your mind.

How big is it?

What does it do?

How does it work?

Your imagination is so powerful!

You can create anything you want in your mind.

Today I'm Going to Be...

Take a long breath in, let it all the way out, and hold your body still.

Think about how you want the rest of your day to go.

Pick a good word to finish this sentence in your mind: "Today, I'm going to be . . ."

KIND

FRIENDLY

HAPPY

HELPFUL

Maybe you finish it with "friendly," or "kind," or "helpful."

Choose a good word that you like to finish the sentence.

When you pick your word, if you want to,
tell a grownup about it.

Remember your word, and do your best to make it happen!

Do you ever feel kind of blaaahhh . . . ? Maybe you feel sleepy, or like you have no energy at all. Then try one of these exercises! They'll get you fired up with plenty of focused energy in no time. At the beginning of each one, sit up tall, take a big breath in, and let it all the way out. Go!

1-2-3 Clap!

Open your arms out really wide.

Count one, two, three . . . and clap your hands one time!

Rub your hands together and make some energy.

Put your hands on your belly. Take a long breath in, and let it all out.

Open your arms out really wide again.

Count one, two, three . . . and clap your hands one time!

Rub those hands together, faster this time. Make some energy!

Put your hands over your heart.

Take a long breath in, and let it all the way out!

53

Bunny Breath

Sit up tall, and hold your body still.

Make bunny paws with your hands.

Take quick, little bunny breaths in through your nose: "sniff, sniff, sniff, sniff!" and then let the air all the way out.

Do it again. Take quick, little bunny breaths in through your nose: "sniff, sniff, sniff, sniff!" and then let the air all the way out.

Now put one hand on your belly. See if you can feel your belly muscles working.

Take quick, little bunny breaths in through your nose: "sniff, sniff, sniff, sniff!" and then let the air all the way out.

Grab a carrot for a snack!

Crrunnch!

Wake Up Your Face!

Open your eyes wide, and blink them three times.

Wiggle your eyebrows up and down.

Wiggle your nose like a bunny!

Open your mouth really wide, and wiggle your jaw back and forth.

Stick your tongue out as far as it will go!

Can you make a fishy face?

Wiggle your whole head around!

Now hold your body still.

Take a long breath in, and let it all the way out!

Twister

Sit up tall, pull your belly in, and make it strong.

Put both hands on your left leg and take a big breath in.

Let the air out, and twist your body to the left. Look over your left shoulder. What do you see?

Breathe in, breathe out, and see you if you can twist to the left a little bit more.

Un-twist your body, so you're looking straight ahead.

Put both hands on your right leg and take a big breath in.

Let the air out, and twist your body to the right. Look over your right shoulder. What do you see?

Breathe in, breathe out, and see you if you can twist to the right a little bit more.

Un-twist your body, so you're looking straight ahead.

Shake your body out a little bit, and then hold still. Take a long breath in, and let it all the way out!

Hot Soup

Imagine you're holding
a hot cup of soup.

It's much too hot
to eat right now!

Breathe in and say,
"It's ha-ha-ha-ha-hot!"

Breathe in and say,
"It's ha-ha-ha-ha-hot!"

Put one hand on your belly,
and see if you can feel your
belly muscles working
as you say it.

Breathe in and say,
"It's ha-ha-ha-ha-hot!"

Put your soup down.

Take a long breath in,
and let it all the way out!

Lion Breath

Imagine you're a sleepy lion, just waking up in the morning.

Make lion claws with your hands. Stretch and wiggle your lion claws all around.

Take a big breath in, and as you let it out, say, "Haaaaahhh!"

Stick your lion tongue out as far as it will go!

Do it again. Take a big breath in and say, "Haaaaahhh!"

Stick that lion tongue out as far as it will go!

Now shake out your lion claws. Take a long breath in, and just let it all the way out.

You're ready to go!

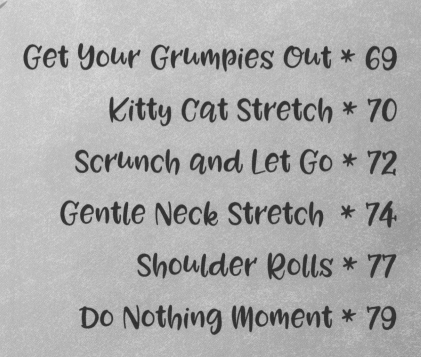

Everybody gets stressed out sometimes. Do you ever feel like that? The exercises here will teach your body *and* your mind to relax and help you let go of that stress. With some practice, it will get easier to relax when you need to. First, sit up tall, hold still, then take a long breath in and a long breath out. Aaahhh . . .

Get Your Grumpies Out

Can you make a grumpy face? I bet you can.
Make a really grumpy face!

Maybe you feel a little sad or angry today.

If you do, make a sad face or an angry face.

Now take a really big breath in, and **blow** all those bad
feelings away!

Do it again, just in case they didn't all go . . .

Take a really big breath in, and **blow** all those bad
feelings away!

Sit up really tall. Maybe smile a little smile . . .

Take another long breath in, and let the air all the way out.

Kitty Cat Stretch

Sit up tall and clasp your fingers together.

Stretch your arms straight out in front of you, and turn your hands so your palms are pressing out away from your body.

Take a big breath in, let the air out, and round your back like a kitty cat stretching.

Meow!

Pull your belly in, and press your hands as far away from you as you can!

Take another big breath in, let the air out, and round your back like a kitty cat stretching.

Meow!

Let your hands go, and give your arms a little shake.

Scrunch and Let Go

Scrunch up your toes, and make all the muscles in your legs *really strong*.

Pull your belly in, and squeeze the muscles in your arms.

Make your hands into fists, and scrunch up your face.

If you want to, squeeze your eyes shut.

Now take a long breath in, and as you let the air out, slowly let all those muscles go.

Take another long breath in, and as you let the air out, let your whole body relax.

Aaahhh . . .

Do it again if you'd like!

Gentle Neck Stretch

Sit up tall and slowly, gently let your head fall to one side.

Breathe in and breathe out.

Sit up tall again and slowly, gently let your head fall to the other side.

Breathe in and breathe out.

Feel how heavy your head is!

Sit up tall once more. Slowly roll your head down toward your belly.

Breathe in and breathe out.

Sit up tall, take another long breath in, and let it all the way out.

Shoulder Rolls

Sit up tall and pull your belly in.

Squeeze your shoulders up as high as you can.
Try to touch your shoulders to your ears!

Take a long breath in. Let it out, and lower
your shoulders down.

Now make circles with your shoulders.

Lift them up, and then press them back.

Lower them down, and then press them forward.

Keep going, rolling your shoulders in a big circle.

Do it one more time. Roll your shoulders
in a big circle.

Now give your shoulders a good
wiggle. Shake 'em out!

Do Nothing Moment

Does it feel like there's always something you're supposed to be doing?

There are places you have to go, and lots of jobs to do.

And everyone seems to be in a hurry!

Well, for this moment, there's nothing you have to do. Except, of course, breathe.

Breathe in, breathe out. If you want, close your eyes.

Breathe in, breathe out.

Breathe in, breathe out.

Conclusion

Remember: Whether you feel tired, grumpy, jumpy, or happy, you can always be mindful. Being mindful just means stopping for a minute to pay attention to what's going on inside of you. And there are lots of fun ways to do it—you can imagine you're a cloud, stretch like a kittycat, or breathe like a bear!

Acknowledgments

I'm so grateful to the many people who worked on this book. Thanks to Eric Wight, the creative and editorial director of Rodale Kids, for his vision from the beginning. Thanks to my wonderful and sunny editor, Anna Cooperberg, and my terrifically smart agent, Allison Cohen. And I can't even imagine the book without illustrator Anni Betts' remarkable, whimsical drawings.

Thanks to the rest of the team at Rodale Kids: publisher Gail Gonzales, editorial director Jennifer Levesque, marketing and PR coordinator Venetia Persaud, marketing and PR consultant Jason Wells, managing editor Sara Cox, project editor Andrea Modica, designer Christina Gaugler, and editorial assistant Kelsey Jopp.

Tons of gratitude to my fantastic assistant, Katie Brennan, and to my family—David, Lola, Tristan, and Brody—for their support.

Finally, a big shout-out to the fabulous Mindy Thomas of Sirius XM Radio's Kids Place Live, who first suggested that I create "Backseat Yoga Breaks" to put on the air. These turned into my children's CD *Mindful Moments for Kids* and eventually became the basis for this book!

About the Author and Illustrator

Kira Willey is an award-winning children's music artist, kids' yoga expert, and creator of Rockin' Yoga school programs. She teaches yoga and mindfulness to children through her music, which has won Parents' Choice Gold and Independent Music Awards. Kira performs her highly popular Rockin' Yoga School Assemblies and Concerts at venues nationwide and leads workshops with teachers and parents to help them incorporate mindful practices into children's daily lives.

Anni Betts is a professional illustrator who creates vibrant, cheerful drawings for books, magazines, advertisements, greeting cards, and more. Originally from Illinois, she now lives in England, with her family.